OUR SOLAR SYSTEM

LEVEL **3** READER

READING LEVEL
3
GRADES 2 TO 4

Copyright ©2010 Creative Edge, LLC. All rights reserved.
Printed in Guangzhou, Guangdong, China.

Written by Kathryn Knight
Special thanks to NASA for information and photos.

The Milky Way

There are many galaxies in the known Universe. Our galaxy is the Milky Way—a beautiful starry spiral with several arms. From Earth we can only see an arm of the Milky Way as it stretches across the sky. It looks like a band of hazy lights. The Milky Way is so wide, it would take a beam of light 150,000 years to go from one side to the other.

Mercury

Venus

Earth

Mars

Sun

Jupiter

OUR SOLAR SYSTEM
- The Sun
- 8 planets: Mercury, Venus, Earth, Mars, Jupiter, Saturn, Uranus, Neptune
- 5 dwarf planets: Ceres, Haumea, Makemake, Pluto, Eris
- Many moons, meteors, comets, asteroids, and interplanetary dust

Our Solar System

The Sagittarius arm of the Milky Way is filled with stars. One of them is our very own Sun. The Sun and all the planets and natural satellites that orbit the Sun make up our Solar System. The Solar System travels in a path around the Milky Way's center. The last time our Solar System was in the same current spot in the Milky Way was during the days of the dinosaurs.

Scientists use huge telescopes to view objects in our Solar System—and beyond. In 1990, the Hubble Space Telescope was launched into orbit. It has sent back incredibly clear images from the far reaches of the Galaxy.

Neptune

Uranus

NASA's spacecraft *Voyager I* was launched in 1977 to explore our Solar System. In 2007, it reached its very edge.

Saturn

Planets to scale. Distances not to scale.

Our Sun

When you see a twinkling star in the night sky, it's hard to imagine that the little bit of light you see comes from a huge ball of hot gas, made mostly of hydrogen and helium. A star "shines" because it is releasing great amounts of energy from its core.

Our own Sun is a star. It is huge and powerful. In fact, 1,300,000 Earths could fit "inside" the Sun. Solar flares (sudden eruptions from the surface of the Sun) release energies that equal millions of hydrogen bombs

The planets travel around the Sun in elliptical (almost circular) orbits. They stay in these orbits due to the pull of the Sun's gravity. Each planet is also affected by the gravitational force of their neighboring planets.

Solar means *of the sun*.

THE SUN

- Distance from Earth (avg): 93 million miles
- Circumference (equatorial): 2.7 million miles (109 times Earth)
- Radius (equatorial): 432,223 miles (109 times Earth)
- Average day length: 609 hours
- Temperature avg: 10,000°F
- Number of planets: 8 planets and 5 dwarf planets
- A 100-pound child would weigh 2,800 pounds on the Sun!

The planet closest to the Sun is Mercury. It's also the smallest. If you were to travel all the way around Mercury at its equator, you would travel 9,525 miles. The same trip around Earth's equator would be 24,902 miles.

Mercury is the fastest-moving planet. While Earth takes 365 days to make a complete orbit around the Sun, Mercury completes a solar revolution every 88 days. Therefore, a year on Mercury is 88 days long. However, though it travels quickly around the Sun, Mercury spins very, very slowly on its axis. It takes 176 Earth days for Mercury to go from "noon to noon"—one day.

The force and pull of gravity is not as strong on Mercury. An object that weighs 100 pounds on Earth would only weigh 38 pounds on Mercury.

MERCURY

- First planet from our Sun.
- Smallest planet in our Solar System
- Distance from Sun (avg): 36 million miles
- Circumference (equatorial): 9,525 miles
- Radius (equatorial): 1,516 miles
- Solar revolution: 88 days
- Average day length: 176 Earth days
- Temperature range: −276/801°F
- Number of moons: 0
- A 100-pound child would weigh 38 pounds on Mercury.

Ancient astronomers knew about Mercury. Early in the morning and just before sunset they could spot an object in the sky. The Greeks believed these were two different planets. The object at sunrise they called Apollo, after the god of the Sun. The object in the early evening they called Hermes, after the messenger of the gods. Later astronomers determined that this was, indeed, only one planet—and it was renamed Mercury, the Roman name for Hermes.

Mercury looks very similar to our Moon. It is barren and rocky, covered with flat areas and deep craters. In 1974, the *Mariner 10* spacecraft reached Mercury and sent back the first close-up images of the surface of Mercury. MESSENGER spacecrafts have been mapping the surface since 2004. NASA hopes to map the entire surface starting in 2011.

Could we live on Mercury? No. Its surface can reach 801°F. That's hot enough to melt lead. In the craters at Mercury's poles, temperatures can fall as low as −276°F. These extremes make Mercury a fun place to study, but not to visit!

The MErcury Surface, Space ENvironment, GEochemistry and Ranging (MESSENGER) probe is a NASA spacecraft, launched August 3, 2004, so named because Mercury is the messenger of the gods.

Venus

The second-closest planet to the Sun is Venus. Its orbit runs between Mercury's and Earth's. It is the brightest object in the sky besides our Sun and the Moon, though it cannot be seen in the middle of the night. At certain times of the year, Venus appears in the eastern sky at sunrise and is called the *morning star*. Certain times at sunset it appears in the western sky and is called the *evening star*. Ancient astronomers first thought these were two different objects.

Venus is called Earth's twin or sister planet because it is almost the same size as Earth, 7,521 miles across—though that's where the similarities end. Venus is a dry, rocky, dusty, waterless planet of vast plains, mountains, canyons, volcanoes, and impact craters.

Venus was named in honor of the **Roman goddess of love and beauty**.

VENUS

- Second planet from our Sun
- Sixth-largest planet in our Solar System
- Distance from Sun (avg): 67 million miles
- Circumference (equatorial): 23,627 miles
- Radius (equatorial): 3,760 miles

- Solar revolution: 225 days
- Average day length: 243 Earth days
- Temperature: 870°F
- Number of moons: 0
- A 100-pound child would weigh 88 pounds on Venus.

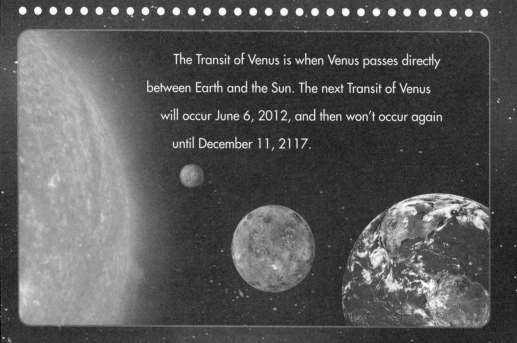

The Transit of Venus is when Venus passes directly between Earth and the Sun. The next Transit of Venus will occur June 6, 2012, and then won't occur again until December 11, 2117.

(Impact craters form when a planet and asteroid collide.) The Maxwell mountain range is about 7 miles high and 540 miles long. It is the highest feature on the planet. In the Beta Regio area there is a canyon just over half a mile deep. Venus also has a 200-mile river of hardened lava. Of all the planets, Venus is the hottest. Venus is covered by thick clouds of sulfuric acid and carbon dioxide that trap the Sun's heat. Its surface averages a scorching 870°F!

Venus rotates very slowly on its axis, so it has a very, very long day—243 Earth days! In fact, it takes longer for Venus to rotate on its axis than for it to travel all the way around the Sun, so its day is longer than its year. Unlike Earth (which rotates from west to east), Venus rotates from east to west. On Venus, the Sun rises in the west and sets in the east.

Earth

Earth, our home, is the third planet from the Sun. It is a compact, solid planet—the densest in the Solar System. The surface of Earth is covered mostly with water. It is the only known planet with life forms and liquid water.

Life on Earth is possible because of our unique atmosphere, made up of layers of gases, held in place by Earth's gravity. This mix of gases, with some water vapor, absorbs ultraviolet radiation from the Sun and keeps the planet from experiencing temperature extremes. There is no defined boundary between Earth's atmosphere and outer space. Our atmosphere simply gets thinner and thinner until it fades into space at about 60 miles above Earth.

EARTH

- Third planet from our Sun
- Fifth-largest planet in our Solar System
- Distance from Sun (avg):
  93 million miles
- Circumference (equatorial): 24,902 miles
- Radius (equatorial): 3,963 miles
- Solar revolution: 365.26 days
- Average day length: 23.93 hours
- Temperature range: −126/136°F
- Number of moons: 1 (Luna)

Earth's Moon (Luna)

The rise and fall of ocean surfaces, which causes low and high tides, is due to the slight gravitational tug of our nearest neighbor and only natural satellite, the Moon. The gray, sandy Moon has many craters and no active volcanoes. We could not live on the Moon without special suits, a source of water, and an air supply—although the Moon's southern pole actually does contain small amounts of water!

EARTH'S MOON

- Distance from Earth (avg): 238,855 miles
- Radius (equatorial): 1,080 miles
- Circumference (equatorial): 6,783 miles
- Average day/year length: 27.32 Earth days
- Temperature range: −387/253°F
- A 100-pound child would weigh 17 pounds on the Moon.

"ONE SMALL STEP FOR MAN, ONE GIANT LEAP FOR MANKIND."

On Sunday, July 20, 1969, Neil Armstrong, of the *Apollo 11* mission, was the first human to set foot on the Moon. He and Edwin "Buzz" Aldrin spent hours exploring the lunar surface while Michael Collins orbited above.

Mars

Mars is the fourth planet from the Sun and is one of Earth's "next-door neighbors" in space. Mars is called the Red Planet. Viewed from Earth, Mars is a bright rusty-red color due to the iron in its soil. Its surface is covered in red dust. Mars has strong winds that kick up small tornados and dust storms that can sometimes swirl over the entire planet. Mars is much colder than Earth, despite its desert-like appearance.

Mars has a rocky surface with deep canyons and high peaks. One canyon is deeper and longer than Earth's Grand Canyon. Some Martian mountains are quite a bit higher than Mount Everest, Earth's highest peak. Mars has the largest volcanoes in

Mars was named for the **Roman god of war.**

MARS

- Fourth planet from our Sun
- Second-smallest planet in our Solar System
- Distance from Sun (avg): 142 million miles
- Circumference (equatorial): 13,263 miles

- Radius (equatorial): 2,111 miles
- Solar revolution: 687 days
- Average day length: 24.6 hours
- Temperature range: −125/23°F
- Number of moons: 2 (Deimos, Phobos)
- A 100-pound child would weigh 38 pounds on Mars.

Mars can be observed through telescopes, but space probes flying past the planet have sent back amazing information about our neighbor. A Mars Pathfinder landed on Mars in 1997 and released a small robot-rover called *Sojourner*. The rover scuttled across Mars' surface, collecting information about rocks, soil, climate, and atmosphere. No human being has ever set foot on Mars—yet!

the solar system. The tallest one, Olympus Mons (Latin for Mount Olympus), rises 17 miles (27 km) from its base. There are also channels and what look like water gullies on Mars. Could water once have flowed on this barren planet? Many scientists think so. Space probes have revealed that frozen water does exist at the Martian polar caps. However, no liquid water has been detected.

Jupiter

Jupiter, the fifth planet from the Sun, is brighter in the night sky than most stars. It is the heaviest and largest planet. It would take more than 1,000 Earths to fill it. Jupiter has the strongest magnetic field of all the planets. Like a giant magnet, it pulls objects into its orbit. Perhaps this is why Jupiter has 63 moons! Its largest moons are Io, Europa, Ganymede, and Callisto—the "Galilean satellites," named for Galileo, the Italian astronomer who discovered them in 1610. Ganymede is larger than the planet Mercury!

This **"King of Planets"** was named for the **Roman king of the gods.**

JUPITER

- Fifth planet from our Sun
- Largest planet in our Solar System
- Distance from Sun (avg): 484 million miles
- Circumference (equatorial): 279,118 miles
- Radius (equatorial): 44,423 miles
- Solar revolution: 12 years
- Average day length: 9.92 hours
- Temperature: −234°F
- Number of moons: 63
- A 100-pound child would weigh 240 pounds on Jupiter.

Unlike Mercury, Venus, Earth, and Mars, Jupiter has very little solid matter. It is one of the "gas giants." Scientists believe that Jupiter, like the Sun, is made primarily of hydrogen and helium. Dense clouds of hydrogen, helium, methane, and ammonia cover its surface with beautiful bands of color. Jupiter also has three thin rings of dust around its equator.

For more than 300 years, astronomers have marveled at Jupiter's Great Red Spot. This is a swirling mass that looks like a hurricane. This storm is almost three times the diameter of Earth. Its outside edge swirls at about 225 miles (360 km) per hour.

Jupiter's year is long. It takes 12 Earth years for Jupiter to complete its orbit around the Sun. However, its day is very fast because it rotates on its axis faster than any planet. It takes a little less than 10 hours to make one rotation, compared with 24 hours for Earth. This rapid spin makes the planet bulge at its equator, so Jupiter is not as round as Earth.

These marks on Jupiter are scars. They were made by the Comet Shoemaker - Levy 9 when it crashed into Jupiter's surface in 1994.

scars

comet

Saturn

Saturn, the sixth planet from the Sun, is the second-largest planet. With its amazing rings, Saturn is one of the most stunning objects in the Solar System. The seven distinct rings (and thinner mini rings, or ringlets) are made of billions of rocks and ice particles. Saturn can be seen in the night sky without a telescope, but its rings cannot. Saturn was the farthest planet that the ancient astronomers knew about.

Like Jupiter, Saturn is a gas giant with no solid surface. It seems to have a hot solid inner core of iron and rock. Its outer core is probably made of ammonia, methane, and water. Saturn's surface and atmosphere contain mostly hydrogen and helium. A dense layer of clouds covers Saturn.

SATURN

- Sixth planet from our Sun
- Second-largest planet in our Solar System
- Distance from Sun (avg): 886 million miles
- Circumference (equatorial): 235,298 miles

- Radius (equatorial): 37,449 miles
- Solar revolution: 29.4 years
- Average day length: 10.66 hours
- Temperature: −288°F
- Number of moons: 62 (Titan is largest.)
- A 100-pound child would weigh 107 pounds on Saturn

Saturn's major rings are very wide. The outermost may measure as much as 180,000 miles (300,000 km) across! The Italian astronomer Galileo first discovered faint images of Saturn's rings in the early 1600s, using a small telescope. In 1656, using a more powerful telescope, Christiaan Huygens, a Dutch astronomer, described a "thin, flat" ring around Saturn. In 1675, Giovanni Domenico Cassini, a French astronomer, described two separate rings made up of swarms of satellites. *Voyager 2* sent back images in 1980 revealing moons, seven rings, and smaller ringlets.

Saturn has at least 62 moons. Its largest, Titan, is larger than Mercury. Titan has a nitrogen-rich atmosphere, similar to ancient Earth's, and could possibly support life forms.

Saturn was named for the **Roman god of agriculture** and strength—the father of Jupiter and Neptune.

In 1997, NASA sent a probe called *Cassini* to study Saturn. It reached Saturn's orbit in 2004. *Cassini* also carried a probe called *Huygens* built by the European Space Agency. *Huygens* separated from *Cassini* and, with a small parachute, landed on Titan, Saturn's largest moon. This is the only landing to take place in the outer Solar System.

Uranus

Uranus is the seventh planet from the Sun, and is the third-largest planet. This beautiful blue planet has several faint rings and at least 27 moons. Although it can be (barely) seen without a telescope, ancient astronomers did not know it was a planet. It was first labeled a planet in 1781 by Sir William Herschel, a British astronomer, who tracked its movement using a telescope. The German astronomer Johann E. Bode named it Uranus after the Greek sky god, Saturn's father.

Replica of the telescope with which Herschel observed Uranus.

URANUS

- Seventh planet from our Sun
- Third-largest planet in our Solar System
- Distance from Sun (avg): 1.78 billion miles
- Circumference (equatorial): 99,787 miles
- Radius (equatorial): 15,882 miles

- Solar revolution: 84 years
- Average day length: 17.24 hours
- Temperature: −357°F
- Number of moons: 27 (Oberon and Titania are the largest.)
- A 100-pound child would weigh 90 pounds on Uranus.

Uranus is a giant ball of gas and liquid. Blue-green clouds of frozen methane cover its surface. Fast winds of up to 500 miles (805 km) per hour rage through its hydrogen-rich atmosphere. Here the temperature may be –357° F, the coldest planetary atmosphere in the Solar System. About 4,700 miles below the clouds there may be an ocean of liquid water and ammonia. Here the temperature may be a scorching 4,200° F, supporting no life forms.

A Uranian year takes just over 84 Earth years. Just as Earth is slightly tilted on its axis, so is Uranus—but Uranus is tilted completely on its side. Astronomers think that Uranus must have been knocked off its axis after a collision with another planet soon after Uranus was formed.

In 1986, the NASA spacecraft *Voyager 2* came within 50,000 miles (80,000 km) of the cloud-cover of Uranus. *Voyager 2* was able to study the Uranian atmosphere and weather patterns. It sent back information on newly discovered moons and rings.

north pole

south pole

Uranus has a number of thin rings, visible in this image taken by the Hubble telescope. Here you can see how Uranus is tilted on its side.

Neptune

    Neptune, the fourth-largest planet, is the farthest planet from the Sun (although there are farther dwarf planets). Neptune's yearly course around the Sun takes 165 Earth years. Like the other giant planets, it is mostly made of gases, hydrogen and helium, along with water and minerals. Thick clouds of frozen methane cover Neptune's surface. Winds up to 700 miles (1,100 km) per hour blow these clouds across the planet. Under the clouds is an atmosphere of thick gases and then a layer of liquid that covers a core of rock and ice. Several dark, faint rings encircle Neptune.

In August 1989, *Voyager 2* provided the first close-up views of Neptune, its faint rings, and its moons.

NEPTUNE

- Eighth (farthest) planet from our Sun
- Fourth-largest planet in our Solar System
- Distance from Sun (avg): 2.8 billion miles
- Circumference (equatorial): 96,683 miles
- Radius (equatorial): 15,388 miles
- Solar revolution: 165 years
- Average day length: 16.11 hours
- Temperature: −353°F
- Number of moons: 13 (Triton is largest.)
- A 100-pound child would weigh 110 pounds on Neptune.

A telescope is needed to view Neptune, yet this is not how Neptune was first "discovered." Instead, it was mathematics that revealed Neptune's presence. Until 1843, astronomers believed Uranus to be the most distant planet. In tracking its orbit and position in the night sky, they noticed that Uranus was not always where they thought it should be. What could cause it to veer from its predicted path? It had to be the force of gravity of some large unknown body—another planet!

In 1843, John C. Adams, a young English astronomer, used mathematics to figure out the distance and position of an object that could affect Uranus' position the way it did. Meanwhile, Urbain J. J. Leverrier, a young French mathematician, was also working on the problem. He predicted the same distance. The findings of both men were put to the test. Astronomers fixed their telescopes and searched that position and distance in the night sky—and *there* was the new planet, exactly as predicted!

Neptune, the deep blue planet, was named for the **Roman god of the sea.**

Neptune has 13 known moons.

Triton, the lower crescent, is its largest.

This image was shot by *Voyager 2*.

Dwarf Planets

● ●

For 76 years, Pluto was known as the ninth planet. In 2006, Pluto was put into a new category: dwarf planet. So, what's the difference between a planet and a dwarf planet? According to the IAU (International Astronomical Union), a planet:

- is an object that orbits our Sun (and is not a moon)
- is large and dense enough to form a sphere
- has "cleared the neighborhood" of its orbit

Pluto does orbit the Sun and form a sphere; but it shares its orbit around the Sun with many, many other objects in its "neighborhood," the Kuiper (KY-per) Belt.

Pluto was discovered in 1930 by **Clyde Tombaugh**. It was named for the **Roman god of the cold, mysterious underworld.**

As of 2010, five objects in our Solar System were listed as dwarf planets (more may be later identified).

Ceres is the smallest and closest to the Sun. It is the largest object in an asteroid belt between Mars and Jupiter.

Pluto is the second largest and second closest to the Sun, located (usually) beyond Neptune in the Kuiper Belt.

Haumea and **Makemake**, also in the Kuiper Belt, are much smaller than Pluto.

Eris, the largest and most distant, is over 9 billion miles from the Sun. It takes 560 Earth years to complete its orbit.

Asteroids, Meteors, and Comets

ASTEROIDS

Many rocky objects, called asteroids, orbit the Sun. Most stay within an asteroid belt between Mars and Jupiter. Asteroids range from a few hundred feet to hundreds of miles across. Some have their own moons.

In 2007, NASA launched a probe called *Dawn Mission* to study some of the largest asteroids. It will reach them during the years 2011–2015.

METEORS

A shooting star is actually a meteor— a piece of rock or iron that has entered Earth's atmosphere. Meteors can break off of asteroids or fall from the tail of a passing comet. Some have even come from the Moon and Mars.

As a meteor falls through our atmosphere, it burns up—most of the time. Sometimes part of the meteor survives the fall and lands on Earth. This chunk is then called a meteorite.

COMETS

A comet trailing across the night sky is a rare and lovely sight. Comets are made of ice, rocks, dust, and gas. Most come from the outer regions of the Solar System and may take hundreds of years to orbit the Sun. As a comet passes near the Sun, its nucleus (center) heats up and sends out a flare—the long tail we see from Earth. A comet's tail can be six million miles long!

Some comets return to within our view every 75 years or so, such as Halley's Comet. Others, like Comet Hale-Bopp, only pass overhead every 2,537 years.

Earthrise

● ●

On Christmas Eve, 1968, the crew of *Apollo 8,* the first manned mission to the Moon, broadcast pictures they had taken of Earth while orbiting the Moon. Astronaut Jim Lovell remarked, "The vast loneliness is awe-inspiring and it makes you realize just what you have back there on Earth."

Our Earth, with its liquid water, atmosphere, and perfect distance from the Sun and Moon, remains unique in all the Solar System. Earth is home to life. Could there be life somewhere else in the Solar System? On Mars? On one of Jupiter's moons? Perhaps—but none has been found yet. Even so, the Sun, planets, moons, asteroids, and comets all create a wondrously amazing and beautiful Solar System—our home in the Universe.